This Notebook Belongs To:

_____

_____

live MORE worry LESS

Time to head back to Amazon to order another book. If you enjoyed this notebook, we hope you will share your opinion by leaving a review on Amazon.
Thank you,
Inspired Lines